BACK TO THE BASICS

JACKIE JOHNSON

Dedication

Most of all I dedicate this book to the *team* aka *"Boss Familia"* God placed in my life to keep me accountable, sane, and stable to complete each God given assignments in my life; My family: *Fab 5 Johnsons*; (Anthony, Mikel, Mi'Kayla, and Mikah). To my co-laborer in this gospel, the Silas to my Paul: *Pastor Umbola Griffin*, and to my Overseer and Spiritual Mother; *Apostle Dorvetta Price* and the entire *TPUM Family.* I LOVE YOU ALL!

In addition, I dedicate this book to every leader, spiritual father/mother, mentor that I ever encountered throughout my journey as a disciple and leader; whither good or bad… you helped make me the woman of God, leader, student, teacher, and change agent I am today.

Table of Contents

Dedication 3

CHAPTER 1 "**First things First**" 5

CHAPTER 2 "**The Holy Bible**" .11

CHAPTER 3 "**Salvation**" 21

CHPATER 4 "**The Holy Spirit**" .35

CHAPTER 5 "**Gifts of the Spirit**". 42

CHAPTER 6 "**The Five-Fold Ministry Office**" 56

CHAPTER 7 "**The Teacher**" 61

CHAPTER 8 "**The Evangelist**" 66

CHAPTER 9 "**The Pastor**" 71

CHAPTER 10 "**The Prophet**" .77

CHAPTER 11 "**The Apostle**" 84

CHAPTER 12 "**Church offices**" 93

1

FIRST THINGS FIRST

When we talk about going back to the "basics"; we're really just saying, "it's time to re-evaluate yourself to make sure that you're living up to the teachings, standards, and instructions that Jesus left for every person that would receive him as their Lord and Savior". Many believers today have become so ambitious and zealous to advance themselves in the work of a minister that they forget the basis of salvation after acceptance is the process of becoming more Christ-like in our thoughts, words, deeds, and actions; and that the heart of every believer should be one of humility and servitude no matter what title is in front of their name.

Often times we are so ready and focused on going deeper and higher that we forget the basic characteristics, integrity, rules, etc. that qualify us to be called believers in the first place. The first things we have to understand, know, and keep in our heart always to remain stable in God is, why we needed and accepted Him into our lives to begin with. Although God created us in His image and likeness something went horribly wrong. The fall of Adam and Eve in the garden affected all mankind for thousands of years. Things became worse for mankind and eventually man became wreckless and out of control to the point that God had to send himself in the flesh in the person of Jesus to save mankind. The price he would have to pay would be agony, ridicule, abandonment, and death.

There were five main reason why Jesus died on the cross in the first place. The first reason being; out of obedience to God the father (*St. John 3:17*) *"For God sent not his Son into the world to condemn the world; but that the world through him might be saved"*. The second reason was to exemplify the ultimate act of love for mankind (*Romans*

5:7-8) "For scarcely for a righteous man will one die: yet peradventure for a good man some would even dare to die. [8] But God commended his love toward us, in that, while we were yet sinners, Christ died for us." Jesus' third reason was to defeat the one thing that continued to separate us from God: which was our sins. He died to give us a clean slate, to give us the right to belong to God *(1 Corinthians 15:55-57) "O death, where is thy sting? O grave, where is thy victory? [56] The sting of death is sin; and the strength of sin is the law. [57] But thanks be to God, which giveth us the victory through our Lord Jesus Christ."* His fourth reason was to ensure that we could have everlasting life through His spirit; which we know as the Holy Spirit or the Holy Ghost (*St. John 3:16*) "*For God so loved the world, that he gave his only begotten Son, that whosoever believeth in him should not perish, but have everlasting life.*" The fifth and final reason was so that mankind could be reconciled back unto him (*Colossians 1:21,22*) "*And you, that were sometime alienated and enemies in your mind by wicked works, yet now hath he reconciled* [22] *In the body of his flesh through death, to present you holy and unblameable and unreproveable in his sight"*. It was always God's plan for mankind to be able to commune with Him daily. As we study the book of Genesis, it becomes clear that God's desire and design for man was to have an intimate existence between creator and creation. However, when sin crept in the garden mankind became separated from its purpose and its God. I'm so glad that he loved us enough to fight for us. God could've just destroyed mankind and started all over again, he could have just chosen to not care anymore; but instead he chose to create a way to win us back from the hands of the enemy, our adversary, satan, the evil one; by sending a payment that was strong enough to pay the cost for all the sins, evil, and wrong doing of mankind as a whole. No matter what level of understanding you have as a believer and disciple of Jesus Christ, in order to have a solid foundation these things should be the basis of your understanding, belief, and knowledge base in order to continue to grow and mature in his word, will, and purpose. It is so important to understand exactly what you believe and why you believe it so that you can properly inform others and so that you can battle the enemy within you that will challenge your faith and belief when trouble and hard times come. (1Peter 3:15) *"But sanctify the Lord God in your hearts: and be ready always to give an answer to every man that ask you a reason of the hope that is in you with meekness and fear".* This is why it is so important that each and every one of us truly seek out God's will as a believer. There are so many people that you will encounter in your everyday life as well as individuals opposing your beliefs and then there will be others trying to persuade you to their belief system and way of living. If you do not truly understand who Jesus was and is, who you are as a result of who he is, what God's plan for humanity was and how that applies to everyone living then you can become confused, dissuaded, and even discouraged. So now that we have discussed the core of how and why we even have the opportunity to be God's child let's move on to the next topic which deals with one of the two main sources of information for every believer.

2

THE HOLY BIBLE

So as you might have guessed based on the last sentence in chapter 1; one of the main sources of information for our belief system is "The Holy Bible". It's also known as "The Good Book" and there's even a famous acronym for it; B(basic) I (instructions) B (before) L (leaving) E (earth). All of those titles are a great representation of the pages within it but there's so much more to it than what we may know or have been taught. I say that because one of the first things I remember memorizing within the church was the "Statement of Faith" and there was a line within the statement that said, "we believe the Bible to be the only inspired and infallible word of God…". Like some of you, I recited that for a whole lot of years when people challenged how I knew who God was, how I knew he was real, or how I knew what pleased God or not. But today after twenty-five years in this life as a disciple of Jesus Christ, studying the bible, communing with him daily, receiving revelation knowledge through the Holy Spirit, becoming a true student as opposed to just being a reader of information, and striving every day to live according to his will and example: I have come to understand that I disagree with that line within the Statement of Faith. The bible is NOT the ONLY INSPIRED word of God. Every God led and spirit filled person that writes a book presents the "Inspired words of God", because whatever is in those pages is information that they obtained through their life experiences, results of exercising instruction from the word of God as well as communicating spiritually with God every day. Therefore, that is what makes their writings inspired by God. The bible is also NOT the INFALLIBLE word of GOD. According to the Merriam-Webster dictionary, the word *infallible* is defined as; *being incapable of error, not liable to mislead, deceive, or disappoint, and incapable of error in defining doctrines touching faith or morals.* The reason it is not infallible is because much of the Bible is the words of man, inspired by God, re-telling of events witnessed, or re-counts of Jesus' exact words spoken. The truth will always be that any book that has been written or interpreted by man's hands has a probability of error somewhere because mankind is not perfect. But I don't want you to take my word for it; let's dive into some facts about the bible and its origins.

There were various authors that wrote the books that compile together to constitute the Bible. They wrote these books under divine inspiration of the Holy Ghost. *(2 Timothy 3:16) "All scripture is given by inspiration of God, and is profitable for doctrine, for reproof, for correction, for instruction in righteousness".* These writings may have been recorded without error but they were translated so many times from (3) languages; Hebrew, Aramaic, and

Greek which were the languages of origin. Most of the Old Testament was written in Hebrew which was the native language of Moses. Hebrew was known as a Semitic language because it was spoken throughout the part of the world that was known as Mesopotamia which is modern day Iraq. Their alphabet in that time consisted of twenty-two letters (no vowels until much later). Both the Old and New Testament was composed over a time span of about 1500 years. Other books of the Old Testament such as; some of Ezra, Daniel, and Jeremiah were written in Aramaic. This is also the language that many scholars believe Jesus himself spoke in. So the Bible has been translated from 3 languages to all six hundred and seventy languages that the bible is now available to be read in.

The New Testament books were written in Greek. However, this was not the ancient Greek language we all assume. This was not the language of the educated or high born nobles; it was the language of common folk, ordinary people known as "Koine Greek". It was the common language of the Eastern Mediterranean and its infiltration into society is believed to be a result of the blending of nations largely impacted by the many conquests of Alexander the Great.

Now this is all about the original written languages of the Bible text but now we have to deal with the fact that there were many other books that are not a part of the Bible you and I read today. So let's deal with the process in which books are added to the Bible. This process is known as being canonized. The word cannon itself is derived from the Hebrew word, *"qaneh"* and the Greek word *"kanon"* which both refers to a measuring rod. This word is used to describe only the books that are officially recognized as inspired of God. Surprisingly, books have not been canonized by one set of people. The earliest cannon list was compiled in Rome around 140 A.D. by a known heretic (one who differs in opinion from an accepted belief or doctrine) named; Marcian.

The term was widely used by those of the Roman Catholic faith to describe those who did not fully agree with the writings and teachings of their church. Marcian's cannon list was not an authorized one because it wasn't approved or recognized by those who followed the beliefs and teachings of Jesus, but it shows you just how far back the idea of a cannon was thought of.

There were three criteria for evaluating if a book that had been presented was acceptable to be admitted to the cannon of the Bible. The first criteria; **Prophetic Authorship** means that in order for a book to be accepted it must have been written by a prophet, apostle, or someone who had a special relationship to a prophet or apostle: such as Mark was to Peter or Luke was to Paul. This was mainly because, only those who had witnessed the events or recorded eyewitness testimony could have their writings considered as "Holy Scripture". The second criteria is **The Witness of The Spirit.** This deals with the appeal to the inner witness of the

Holy Spirit within each leader. When the books were being presented to complete the Bible's cannon; scholars that were both believers and unbelievers along with religious leaders were assembled to examine them, and only the books that could be agreed upon as authentic were presented for the last criteria. The last criteria is; **Acceptance**. The last test to determine if the book was authentic was determined by the book's acceptance among followers/believers of Jesus Christ. The assembly of followers would accept or deny the accuracy and reliability of the chosen books through the indwelling of God's Spirit within as well as if the writings were conducive to what was known about Jesus. The official Old Testament Cannon was determined in the fifth century B.C. This cannon consists of the thirty-nine books we read today *(Genesis, Exodus, Leviticus, Numbers, Deuteronomy, Joshua, Judges, Ruth, 1 Samuel, 2 Samuel, 1 Kings, 2 Kings, 1 Chronicles, 2 Chronicles, Ezra, Nehemiah, Esther, Job, Psalm, Proverbs, Ecclesiastics, Song of Solomon, Isaiah, Jeremiah, Lamentations, Ezekiel, Daniel, Hosea, Joel, Amos, Obadiah, Jonah, Micah, Nahum,*

Habakkuk, Zephaniah, Haggai, Zechariah, Malachi). The New Testament Cannon became official in the second century A.D.: which are the twenty-seven books that we accept today, *(Matthew, Mark, Luke, John, Acts, Romans, 1 Corinthians, 2 Corinthians, Galatians, Ephesians, Philippians, Colossians, 1 Thessalonians, 2 Thessalonians, 1 Timothy, 2 Timothy, Titus, Philemon, Hebrews, James, 1 Peter, 2 Peter, 1 John, 2 John, 3 John, Jude, Revelation).*

Although the cannon list was deemed official; not everyone agreed and it is because of that very reason that today; the Protestant bible consist of the thirty-nine Old Testament books. The order of the books is different from the Christian cannon *(Genesis, Exodus, Leviticus, Numbers, Deuteronomy, Joshua, Judges, Ruth, Samuel, Kings, Chronicles, Ezra-Nehemiah, Esther, Job, Psalm, Proverbs, Ecclesiastics, Song of Songs, Isaiah, Jeremiah, Lamentations, Ezekiel, Daniel, Hosea, Joel, Amos, Obadiah, Jonah, Micah, Nahum, Habakkuk, Zephaniah, Haggai, Zechariah, Malachi).* The Protestant bible does also include the twenty-seven New Testament books. The

Hebrew bible which is also known as the "Tanakh" only contains twenty-four books *(Genesis, Exodus, Leviticus, Numbers, Deuteronomy, Joshua, Judges, Samuel, Kings, Isaiah, Jeremiah, Ezekiel, the writings of Kethubim {contains all 12 minor prophet books}, Psalms "Tehilim", Proverbs "Mishlei", Job "Iyov", Song of Songs "Shir HaShirim", Ruth "Rus", Lamentations "Eicha", Ecclesiastics "Kohelese", Esther, Daniel "Doniel", Ezra/Nehemiah, Chronicles "Divrei Hayamim".* The Judaism bible only acknowledge the Torah *(Genesis, Exodus, Leviticus, Numbers, Deuteronomy).* These five books are also known as the "*Law of Moses*". The Judaism religion in addition to the Torah study a book called the "Talmud". This book is a collection of writings that cover the full gamut of Jewish law and traditions. Lastly, the Roman Catholic bible contains all sixty-six books of the Christian Bible with the addition a set of the "Lost Books" known as the Apocrypha. The "Lost Books" that make up the Apocrypha are; 1 Esdras, 2nd Esdras, Book of Tobit, Book of Judith, Book of Wisdom, Ecclesiasticus, Baruch, Susanna, 1st Maccabees, 2nd

Maccabees, and Rest of Esther). There are over twenty-three lost books and although they have not been accepted into the official cannon of the Bible; there were many of the lost books that were read and practiced by the early churches. These books included: Book of Jubilees, Epistle of Barnabas, Shepherd of Hermas, Paul's Epistle to the Ladioceans, 1 Clement, 2 Clement, Preaching of Peter, Apocalypse of Peter, Gospel according to the Egyptians, and the Gospel according to the Hebrews.

With all of this information regarding the bible, it's translations, and its cannon you can see just how confusing and how easy it is for un informed individuals both in and outside of the faith to make assumptions and errors concerning our Holy Scriptures. This is why it is our belief that having a relationship with the "God of the Bible" is what will be most helpful in your daily understanding, wisdom, and direction for righteous and holy living as a true disciple of Jesus Christ.

3

SALVATION

In many biblically based cultures we use the word "saved" instead of salvation. The word saved really embodies what happens when one receives salvation. However, this can be confusing when trying to minister/witness to others who are unfamiliar with God or "Christian culture". When we become disciples of Jesus Christ and we began to gain experience in practicing holy living we take on the jargon that comes with the culture, but as leaders we have to be able to make things plain to those we are called to help bring into the light of God's infinite will for mankind. To do this effectively, we must learn to define and understand the foundations of our beliefs.

The word "salvation" according to the Merriam-Webster English Dictionary is defined as; a deliverance from the power and effects of sin 2) liberation from ignorance or illusion 3) preservation from destruction or failure; deliverance from danger or difficulty. Salvation is Latin in origin "salvare" which means {to save}. The Greek word "soteria" meaning {deliverance, salvation}. So just as the definition of origin suggest; salvation is the process in which one has been saved from destruction, ignorance, danger, difficulty, and failure. When receive Christ into our hearts and our lives we embark upon a journey and a life that continuously saves us from those things; time after time. Salvation doesn't exclude us from trial, hardship, tragedy, etc. It provides a constant and consistent way for us to be delivered from the hardships, trials, tragedies we may have to face.

Many people do not understand the importance or even the need for salvation. If we are to teach and help others to understand why salvation is needed, we first must understand and know for ourselves. From the beginning of mankind's creation into this world; we existed to worship and commune (have intimate conversation and relationship) with God our creator. In Genesis 1:26-2:18 it clearly outlines God's process of creating man as well as the function and duties he was responsible for. These duties were not extensive as God wanted ample time with Adam every day to walk and talk with him. In Genesis 2:18 God decides that Adam needs a helper/companion that can be with him outside of their daily time. He gave him a mate that could help him with his earthly duties and day to day functions. Man and woman had a peaceful paradise existence. Everything they needed was provided for them in the garden that God created for them. Their only job was to maintain it as well as ruling over it and the animals.

True to human nature; Adam and Eve forfeited their paradise existence due to curiosity and weakness. The one rule God gave to Adam, "do not eat from the tree of the knowledge of life and death in the middle of the garden", is of course the rule they broke because Eve allowed the serpent to create doubt and curiosity within her. Adam's weakness was exhibited when he stood by as the serpent spoke to his wife, didn't stop him from speaking against what God told him, and lastly when he ate with his wife knowing what their fate would be. This event is known as, "the fall of man".

Their consequences for their disobedience within the garden was a life outside of God's paradise. Where man once had it easy; he now was forced to work hard to exist and provide for his wife and children. The woman now had to endure great pain in child birth. And it is here in the consequences of her disobedient that God says; your husband will "rule over you" and be responsible for you. This is a big thing here because God created woman to be equal with her husband but the curse of their disobedience demoted her.

Adam's punishment for his part in the fall consisted of God cursing the ground. This meant that the food would no longer grow on its own and just be there for them to pick and eat. Man would now have to harvest the crops in the ground. He would now have to work hard to make the ground ready, properly tend to it so that it would grow, and then harvest (pick/pluck it and gather it) so they would have food. Then God did one last kindness before expelling them from paradise. He made them clothes from the animal's skin to clothe them.

I went through the details of mankind's fall because that is the reason why all need salvation. Since the day man and woman was put out of the garden (God's ordained place of living for them) mankind has existed under those curses. That was the day that the war with satan began. But because of God's love for mankind; he had to compile a plan to redeem us back from the curse. Nothing would be strong enough to break the curse except his own blood. This is why Jesus was sent in the flesh just like mankind. He would become a living example of what it meant to embody the Spirit of God within. He would experience the trials and hardships of life as all mankind had experienced; to show us that it was possible to live a godly lifestyle even within the evil state of our fleshly shells. And he came to suffer persecution, die, and defeat satan as he rose from the dead. This simply signified the fact that he took on our pain, shame, excuses, etc. to erase the line we couldn't cross. God's act of love, caused him to send his only begotten son as a sacrifice to save us from the destruction, danger, ignorance of sin. To each person that receives the salvation that Jesus died to provide he/she now embarks on a journey of re-discovering what it means to live in the original plan of God.

Now that we know what salvation is and what its purpose is, let's clearly outline how one can receive salvation.

Romans 10:9-10 says, *"that if thou shalt confess with thy mouth the Lord Jesus, and shalt believe in thine heart that God hath raised him from the dead, thou shalt be saved. 10 For with the heart man believeth unto righteousness; and with the mouth confession is made unto salvation."* So plainly put a person receives salvation by truly believing and confessing that Jesus lived on this earth to be an example, died to pay the cost for their sins, and rose to be able to give them the right to receive the indwelling of God's spirit; which gives them the power to overcome sin daily in their lives.

Maintaining salvation is a daily process. If sin separates us from God; then the focus of maintaining one's salvation involves everything that you can do to keep you away from sin and close to God. Romans 12:1-2 says, *"I beseech [beg] you therefore, brethren, by the mercies of God, that ye present your bodies a living sacrifice, holy, acceptable unto God, which is your reasonable service. 2. And be not conformed to this world: but be ye transformed by the renewing of your mind, that ye may prove what is that good, and acceptable, and perfect will of God."*

The process of transformation is not instantaneous in every area of your life. Some things will change immediately because it is within your power to change; other things will require the knowledge, wisdom, and instruction of God to show you how to overcome or be delivered from it. This is why a holy lifestyle is the key component for all believers. The more a person grows and develops within their journey as a believer; God will give specific instruction and guidance designed specifically for them. But before you get to that point of development there are basic truths for all of us to follow that will keep us focused and operating within God's written will.

The first thing you can do is; understand and strive daily to keep God first and become devoted to discovering and following his will: Matthew 6:33 says, *"Seek ye first the Kingdom of God and all these things shall be added unto you."* We must understand that seeking God and keeping him first will cause us to be given everything else we need and seek.

Secondly, it's important to develop a consistent prayer life. Prayer is how we communicate with God. Notice I said communicate with and not talk to. Communication means there's a dialogue happening; a back and forth if you will. Let us remember that from the beginning God had daily communication with man in the garden, so once you receive salvation and are working your way back to God's perfect design from the beginning; consistent prayer becomes the manifestations of "walking in the garden with God in the cool of the day". Jesus himself when he was on the earth in the flesh prayed consistently to God his father for direction and on behalf of others. We too must pray for direction and on behalf of others. In John 5:30, Jesus says, *"I can of mine own self do nothing: as I hear, I judge: and my judgment is just; because I seek not mine own will, but the will of the Father which hath sent me."*

Thirdly, you must read/study the Holy Scriptures "God's word" daily. The reason we study the word of God is twofold. One reason can be found within John 5:9, *"Search the scriptures; for in them ye think ye have eternal life: and they are they which testify of me"*. This scripture informs us that the key to eternal life with God must be obtained through his word. It is for this reason that he challenges us to not just read the scriptures; but to search (study) them so that we are not misinformed but rather we can be sure that our lives are lined up to his written will, which will ensure that we reign eternally with him.

The next purpose of reading the scriptures can be found within 2 Timothy 2:15, *"Study to shew thyself approved unto God, a workman that needeth not to be ashamed, rightly dividing the word of truth"*. We must study the scriptures so that we can discern the truth within the pages. This scripture lets us know that studying the scriptures and obtaining the truth of the text's meaning (rightly dividing the word of truth) will cause us to not be embarrassed. I Peter 3:*15 "But sanctify the Lord God in your hearts: and be ready always to give an answer to every man that asketh you a reason of the hope that is in you with meekness and fear:"*

This scripture passage helps us to understand that others will want to know why you follow Jesus. They will want to know why your life is different from theirs. According to this passage we must be able to give them an answer; and the goal for every believer is to give them a truthful answer that causes them to want to know your God and follow Jesus for themselves.

Another thing that helps you maintain salvation is; Fellowshipping with other believers. Most believers choose to do this by attending church services. Hebrews 10:24-25, *"And let us consider one another to provoke unto love and to good works: 25) Not forsaking the assembling of ourselves together, as the manner of some is; but exhorting one another: and so much the more, as ye see the day approaching."* However, let us be clear that church attendance does not save nor condemn anyone. In the resurrection of the New Testament church "body of believers" Jesus himself gathered the people together on the sea shores, mountains, and even boat to preach the gospel of

Jesus to them; and many received him. He did not use the temple (our modern day churches) to preach, heal, and deliver. Jesus took his ministry to those who needed him most within the streets of the city. This should inspire us to take "church" everywhere we go. This of course in no means cancels or demeans church attendance. Church attendance within the right congregation of believers is a great tool in assisting believers with enhancement and maturity within their walk with God. It will provide hope and inspiration as well as instruction from more experienced believers on how to effectively navigate life God's way. That fellowship is priceless when done under submission and direction of the Holy Spirit.

Fellowshipping with other believers however is not confined to just attending church services, conferences, etc. The scriptures tell us that the man that wins souls is wise. To fellowship is simply to spend time with someone. There are also several instances within scripture (Mark 2:13-17,

Matthew 9:11, Matthew 14:17-21, Luke 14:1) where Jesus' fellowship consisted of sharing a meal and conversation with others. This practice that seemed to be unorthodox to religious leaders was common practice for Jesus; therefore, it should be the uncommon practices that we use to fellowship with those who need to experience a God encounter.

Lastly, it is important that you continue to follow Jesus no matter what difficulties and struggles you have to face. You have to have realistic expectations of what it means to follow Christ. There are so many people who are told that once they accept Jesus their lives are going to be good and everything is going to work good and smoothly; but that is far from the truth. Following Christ means that you must expect opposition, trials, tribulations, constant warfare, etc. simply because you become a target to satan your enemy when you join the winning side (God's side). Matthew 16:24, *"Then said Jesus unto his disciples, If any man will come after me, let him deny himself, and take up his cross, and follow me."* You have to be done doing whatever "you" want to do. Your life as a follower of Jesus is all about pleasing God. That can be difficult for some because of the selfish and self-centered nature of man. However, to really follow him you have to deny yourself the things your flesh may desire; but God has said "no" to. Reflect back once again to Adam and Eve in the garden: Adam was told not to eat of that particular tree, but he did not deny himself when the temptation presented itself through his wife. He instead chose to give in to his desire to possess knowledge that God said he didn't need to have.

4

THE HOLY GHOST

Receiving salvation is only half the battle as a believer because maintaining your salvation is extremely important. We just discussed the basic/main ways to do this, but more is still required of us after receiving the deliverance of Jesus Christ into our lives. If we truly intend to stay delivered and continue on our daily journey of living for Christ we must receive the indwelling of the Holy Spirit. We must receive the Holy spirit for many reasons. We must receive it because in order to truly live a godly lifestyle we will need God's power working within us to defy our flesh daily. Ephesians 3:20, *"Now unto him that is able to do exceeding abundantly above all that we ask or think, according to the power that worketh in us,"* the power he's referring to is that of the Holy Spirit. According to the scriptures; when we receive the Holy spirit it gives us "power". Acts 1:8, *"But ye shall receive power after that the Holy Ghost is come upon you: and ye shall be witnesses unto me both in Jerusalem, and in all Judaea, and in Samaria, and unto the uttermost part of the earth."*

There are many debates regarding how you receive the Holy Spirit. For instance; I grew up being taught about tarrying. To tarry for the Holy Spirit meant that you would gather (usually at the altar) with others seeking to receive it. You would be partnered with or overseen by a seasoned believer in Christ who was filled with the indwelling of the Holy Spirit already. They would tell you to focus your mind only on God and the things of God. They would tell you to repent of all of your sins so that you could spiritually be clean for the Spirit of God to come inside you and live. Then they would tell you to call on the name of Jesus. Some people received the indwelling quickly, others would have to partake in this service several times before getting it.

Today there are many who oppose this method and feel that it was just a form of working up people's emotions.

Although I personally didn't receive the Holy Spirit this way; I do understand what they were trying to accomplish. They were simply letting you know that in order to receive the indwelling of God's Spirit you had to really desire it; more than anything, you had to be focused on God because the enemy would try to cloud your mind with doubt/fear/and distractions, they had you call on Jesus because the scriptures says that there is power in his name; so calling his name would bring his power "The Holy Ghost", and the fact that others were there and that person was saying it with you gave you the comfortability of allowing yourself to let go enough to be open to receive it.

However, we always have to refer back to the scriptures "God's inspired word" to help us understand the truth of a matter. According to scripture texts there are four ways to receive the indwelling of the Holy Spirit. Ephesians 1:13,

"In whom ye also trusted, after that ye heard the word of truth, the gospel of your salvation: in whom also after that ye believed, ye were sealed with that holy Spirit of promise," This text informs us that the Holy Spirit can be received only after we have believed the message of truth concerning Christ and received salvation are we able to be filled with the Holy Spirit. There are some who will argue that this scripture means that once you receive salvation you are given the Holy Spirit automatically.

The scriptures teach us that the gift of the Holy Spirit can be received after repentance and baptism. Acts 2:38, *"Then Peter said unto them, Repent, and be baptized every one of you in the name of Jesus Christ for the remission of sins, and ye shall receive the gift of the Holy Ghost."* Scripture also says that the Holy Ghost can be received by the laying on of hands in Acts 19:6, *"And when Paul had laid his hands upon them, the Holy Ghost came on them; and they spake with tongues, and prophesied."* Lastly, Luke 11:13 tells us that we can receive the Holy Ghost by simply asking; *"If ye then, being evil, know how to give good gifts unto your children: how much more shall [your] heavenly Father give the Holy Spirit to them that ask him?"* You may be asking the question within your mind; which way is the correct way? The truth is; the bible doesn't give us one particular way that we receive the indwelling of the Holy Ghost; therefore, all of these ways outlined in scripture are avenues God can use to fill you with His Spirit. I personally believe that it's determined by each individual's experience/encounter with God.

I received the Holy Spirit by asking him to dwell within me. I didn't tarry, no one laid hands on me, I got it before being water baptized, and I received it one day after receiving salvation. I have also observed individuals who received the indwelling after someone, full of God's power laid their hands on them and prayed for it to come upon them.

There is another controversial discussion that has recently become a huge debate amongst different denominations; that topic is "inclusion". Many spiritual leaders are teaching the doctrine of "inclusion" which states, "once saved, always saved". This of course is untrue because as human beings; we will always have the power of free will. Free will means that we have the right to choose our own path, beliefs, etc. without being forced by God; even to do what is right. A person who has accepted Jesus Christ and confessed him as Lord can indeed choose to in a sense; unaccept him as well. We have seen this happen to many people following God but have experienced great tragedy or loss. In these tragic instances sometimes a person can lose their faith and eventually be so angry with God's decision to allow the loss or tragedy that they denounce him altogether. Therefore, that individual would not be saved any longer.

However, when it comes to the Holy Spirit there is no scripture that tells us God will leave us if we sin. I heard a phrase all of my saved life, "the Holy Ghost will not dwell in an unclean temple". I believed all of that time that this was a scripture passage, but when I searched to find where it was located after advising someone else that the Holy Ghost would leave them if they continued in a sinful lifestyle. I could not find that scripture anywhere and it was because; it just wasn't in the bible. As believers it is extremely important that we do not add or take away things from God's word; just because you feel one way or think a certain way; doesn't make it God's way. What we do know about the Holy Ghost in us is; that our bodies are his dwelling place and we no longer belong to ourselves. 1 Corinthians 6:19-20 says, *"What? Know ye not that your body is the temple of the Holy Ghost which is in you, which ye have of God, and ye are not your own? 20) For ye were bought with a price; therefore, glorify God in your body and in your spirit, which are God's"*. We also know that according to David's writings in Psalm 139:7-8 that God's Spirit cannot be escaped when he dwells within you. David says in this passage, *"Whither shall I go from thy spirit? Or whither shall I flee from thy presence? 8) If I ascend up into heaven, thou art there: if I make my bed in hell, behold, thou art there."*

5

SPIRITUAL GIFTS

The first thing that should be cleared up regarding spiritual gifts is the fact that it is not the same as the "gift of the Holy Spirit". The Holy Spirit is a "gift" in the context that it is freely given to us through God's love for us and our desire to receive it; but the Holy Spirit is the spirit "character" of God. The Holy Spirit is the one that assigns spiritual gifts to each individual. The word gift in the Greek translation is "charismata" which means gift of grace. This definition refers to the special abilities that God has given each believer through His Spirit.

We must also know that a spiritual gift is also not the same thing as natural "talents". Although God can turn our talents into a spiritual gift by placing his supernatural power upon our natural talents to help us establish, promote, and build his kingdom here on earth; we must always remember that they are different. For example: a person who doesn't have the Holy Spirit can have a talent to sing. When they open their mouth you can feel the power or pain within every note; it can wow you or leave you speechless. But a person who has the Holy Spirit within them that possess that same singing talent can cause a person to come to repentance, drive out evil spirits, cause deliverance to take place, or simply allow someone to feel God's presence through their song.

In 1 Corinthians 12: 1 Paul emphasizes that he didn't want the brethren to be ignorant concerning spiritual gifts, so this chapter deals with a list of spiritual gifts (for many scholars believe there are more that are not specifically listed). It also explains that every spiritual gift is distributed to believers through the Holy Spirit. We learn through this chapter that there are many different operations of spiritual gifts; but that they all come from God and are to be used for God. 1 Corinthians 12: 4-6; *"Now there are diversities of gifts, but the same Spirit. 5) And there are differences of administrations, but the same Lord. 6) And there are diversities of operations, but it is the same God which worketh all in all."* 1 Corinthians 12:8-10 gives us a list of nine spiritual gifts: word of wisdom, word of knowledge, faith, gifts of healing, working of miracles, prophecy, discerning of spirits, divers kinds of tongues, interpretation of tongues. Many believers use their spiritual gifts without even understanding exactly what they are; others are seeking and searching to discover what spiritual gifts they have. Let's break down each of these nine gifts so that you may have a more detailed list of things to look for.

Word of wisdom is simple to explain; it's the ability to be able to properly apply the knowledge that you already possess to life situations. This gift is often times confused for "word of knowledge". **Word of knowledge** is supernatural knowledge and insight that's given to you from the Holy Spirit directly. It has nothing to do with the natural knowledge you possess from the things you learn. An example of the word of knowledge in operation would be; me never being trained in carpentry, not having directions but God giving me step by step instructions to build a cabinet. It's all about having knowledge about something that you haven't learned or been taught. My uncle and my youngest son both manifest this gift. My son is only thirteen years old but all of his life he has been able to duplicate anything he sees with paper and other objects. This spiritual gifting caused us to nickname him, "The Architect". but just remember that wisdom is understanding how to effectively apply what you to know and knowledge is "what you know'.

The next spiritual gift is **Faith**. The spiritual gift of faith is not to be confused with the measure of faith that every believer possesses according to Romans 12:3, *"For I say, through the grace given unto me, to every man that is among you, not to think of himself more highly than he ought to think; but to think*

soberly, according as God hath dealt to every man the measure of faith."
This measure of faith is what allows us to receive salvation
in the first place. No one can receive the saving grace of
Jesus Christ without believing that He is the son of God and
that He died on the cross to pay for our sins.

The gift of faith is the supernatural measure of faith that
allows you to believe God for the impossible. This is one of
the most powerful gifts. This gift gives the individual the
ability to trust God to move even in extraordinary and the
most complicated of situations. Romans 10:17, *"So then faith*
cometh by hearing, and hearing by the word of God." A person can
obtain the gift of faith by studying God's word frequently
because God's promises become alive or more real to us as
we discover the range of God's power and true capabilities
as they are revealed within the scriptures. Reading about a
God who has healed the sick, cast out demons, performed
miraculous feats, etc. make the miraculous a reality and not
just a story or words on a page.

Many believe that the gift of faith goes hand in hand with the gifts of healing and the working of miracles. The **gifts of healing** are plural (most people don't catch that) which denotes that there is more than one operation of the gift. Scholars add that it's plural because it can be received both physically and spiritually; and it can happen instantly as well as gradually.

The woman with the issue of blood had suffered many years; but when she touched the hem of Jesus' garment, she was immediately made whole (Matthew 9:20-22). The woman's healing was an example of an immediate manifestation. However, do you remember the story of the blind man in (Mark 8:23-25)? Jesus spat in the man's eye, laid hands on him, and asked if he could see; the man replied that he saw men as trees walking. Jesus then laid his hands on him once more and the man was able to see clearly. That man's healing gradually happened.

Healing means that what is broken is restored and what is sick is made well; throughout scripture we see different ways the gift of healing worked. With the example of the blind man I just gave; he was healed through the laying on of hands. The woman with the issue of blood was healed through her faith in God's ability to heal her, and in (Acts 5:15) It was even believed that the very shadow of the Apostles could bring healing to someone in their path.

Our next gift of the spirit is the **working of miracles**. This is a gift we all secretly long for. This gift is the supernatural ability to perform occurrences against the laws of nature. An example of this gift is when God allowed Moses to turn water into blood in demonstration before Pharaoh in (Genesis 7:20). The walls of Jericho falling down when Joshua led the children of Israel on a seven-day march around it. These are both examples of occurrences that were against the law of nature (Joshua 6:20). Miracles in its truest form are direct products of God's word. (Psalm

33:6) lets us know that it was by God's word that the heavens and earth were made. A person with this gift can use the word of God to speak and cause miracles to happen.

The **gift of divers tongues** can be both confusing and controversial because different kinds of tongues are presented within scripture: **1) tongues unto God**: which is also known as your "heavenly language". 1 Corinthians 14:2 says, *"For he that speaketh in an unknown tongue speaketh not unto men, but unto God: for no man understandeth him; howbeit in the spirit he speaketh mysteries."* **2) tongues as a sign to the unbeliever**: Acts 2:7-8 *"And they were all amazed and marveled, saying one to another, Behold, are not all these which speak Galileans? 8) And how hear we every man in our own tongue, wherein we were born?"* **3) tongues that edify the body**: these tongues are the operation of the gift of tongues. 1 Corinthians 14:5, *"I would that ye all spake with tongues but rather that ye prophesied: for greater is he that prophesieth than he that speaketh with tongues, except he interprets, that the church may receive edifying."* Individuals should never dismiss the value of speaking in tongues for

Paul himself in the above scripture said he wish that all would speak. Paul also instructs the church at Corinth to not forbid tongues from being spoken; but he also advises them to do all things decently and in order. This is not man's order but rather God's order. The variations of tongues and their functions allow us to see that there are specific places and times for each tongue; and Paul was simply verifying that in 1 Corinthians 14:39.

The **interpretation of tongues** was touched on as well in the above scripture. This gift works hand in hand with the gift of diverse tongues. Many traditional tongues have banned speaking within their churches because they view it as confusion; citing that there is no interpreter most times so it is not beneficial to spoken in the church. Other leaders feel that it confuses and frightens un-believers when they come into the church to visit. These practices are wrong and unfair to believers that have reached an intimacy with God that allows them to communicate mysteries. You should never limit your God encounter to pacify others. Now are there ever times when speaking in tongues become disruptive? My answer would be yes; when someone who doesn't truly have that type of intimacy with God tries to manufacture tongues it will go horribly wrong. Some people believe they must convince others that they have a godly relationship, some may feel the pressure of the fact that most believers around them speak in tongues, and others are criticized for not speaking. We as disciples of Jesus Christ must stop judging the progress of one another. It is so important that we understand the different variations of tongues and understand their purpose so that we may help others to understand when something is in order or not. In all things, "try the spirit by the spirit and see if it be the spirit of God"!

The last two spiritual gifts listed are **prophecy** and **discerning of spirits**. We will begin with discerning of spirits; this gift may have been interpreted as "a gut feeling", "an inkling", "psychic ability", "intuition", etc. before you came into the knowledge and acceptance of Christ as your Lord and Savior. Discerning of spirits allow you to perceive the source of a manifestations. It allows the individual to know if the spiritual manifestation (outward action) is from God, man, or the devil. The key word in its name is "spirits". There are only three types of spirits; demons, ministering spirits "angels", and human spirits "flesh". In every action that happens daily; one of the three are operating. This gift allows you to know which is in operation. Every believer that has received the Holy Spirit has the ability to discern through the power of God; but for someone with these gifts, it comes easier or more natural.

If you read the scripture text of Acts 8:18-23 you will see how a man named Simon offered the Apostles money to give him the power, they possessed. The power that allowed them to lay hands on people and they received the Holy Spirit. Paul's gift of discernment allowed him to see that

Simon's heart and intentions were not right; this leads Paul to tell Simon to repent for his wickedness so that the thoughts of his heart could be forgiven. This gift is important because evil often times masquerades as good; 2 Corinthians 11:13-14 *"For such are false apostles, deceitful workers, transforming themselves into the apostles of Christ. 14) And no marvel; for satan himself is transformed into an angel of light."* This gift is essential to the purity and survival of the body of believers. Individuals with this gift are not very popular and may often times be misunderstood or mistaken to be judgmental; but we cannot survive without them because they are the measuring sticks of the spirit. This gift allows us to know the difference between the real and the fake, the evil and the godly, the prophecy and the lie.

Our last and most coveted gift is prophecy. There are many misconceptions regarding this gift so let's jump right into the facts. The gift of prophecy is NOT the same as walking in the five-fold office of the prophet. We will discuss the office of a prophet in great detail in our next chapter. The gift of prophecy is to bring forth an inspired utterance. The Holy Ghost reveals the heart of God through a thought, a vision, or an audible voice. 1 Corinthians 14:3 *"But he that prophesieth speaketh unto men to edification, and exhortation, and comfort."* The gift of prophecy is to edify the church "body of believers as a whole" as well as unbelievers. It is a sign that God is truly among us. The individuals that possess this gift are sensitive to the unction of the Holy Ghost as well as the needs of the body of believers. These individuals should be diligent students of God's word because it is by his word that they should test/examine their prophetic utterance to ensure that it will build up the body of Christ. expected to be followed by confirmation to ensure the person is not speaking from any other source than the Holy Spirit. Although the prophet and individuals that have the gift of prophecy are able to operate the same in many instances there are a few distinct differences between them.

I guess all I'm really trying to say is; having the gift of prophecy doesn't make you a prophet.

6

THE FIVE-FOLD OFFICES

Ephesians 4:11-12 gives us the purpose for the five-fold ministry offices; *"And he gave some, apostles; and some prophets; and some, evangelist; and some, pastors and teachers; 12) For the perfecting of the saints, for the work of the ministry, for the edifying of the body of Christ:"* This scripture text clearly lets us know that there are three purposes for the five-fold ministry offices to exist. The first reason is to perfect the saints. This simply means that they exist as leaders to help the believer with their growth and development. The second function of the five-fold is to catapult the work of the ministry. This means that physical work must be done to enhance the "kingdom agenda". No person who holds any of these five offices should be found not "working". Preaching is not the only work to be done. All believers (but especially leaders) have an obligation to be an example to others of who God is, his love for us, and his divine order of livelihood for all saints. This is not done by word only; it must be done by precept and example. This means that what we say should mirror what we do. Our actions show everyday people just who our God is. This is why Matthew 5:16, *"Let your light so shine before men, that they may see your good works, and glorify your Father which is in heaven."*.

The work of the ministry includes serving God and His church (body of believers) in their various areas of need. It includes not just ministering the word but, keeping order amongst the saints. This is a job that will not always be a smooth, easy, non-confrontational, non-offensive job to do. It also included the tasks of maintaining your own discipline and lifestyle practices, to ensure they match up to scriptural teaching. The last purpose of the five-fold is; the edifying of the body of Christ. It is extremely important that when you observe any text within the bible; where it speaks of the "body of Christ" you understand that we are not speaking of the synagogue/temple/church building. Too often leaders have taught people to reverence the building but not be the "body"; it is for this reason that most people stay in dead churches and under wrong leadership; even though they recognize that they're not growing or maturing in God.

The building is not the church; no matter how many people get angry about hearing that; it's true. Jesus himself rarely went into the actual temple and when he did; it was to perform some miracle, to teach, to correct. Not once did he enter the temple to worship or partake in their worship experience. Now, don't be alarmed or confused by this: many times Jesus recognized that the temples belonged to man because they did not revere him; they didn't even believe he had come so how could they receive him? We as saints believe in church; but make sure that you're attending a church body with leaders that are obedient to God, seek him for His direction concerning the body of believers, and live a submitted godly lifestyle; because if they're not you are just attending a social club.

We build the body through love, faith, and teaching the universal principles of godly living; to assist both existing believers as well as those who are new to their walk. Teaching others about Christ, living a godly lifestyle, and being a consistent part of their life are all the basic fundamentals of how we truly welcome people into "THE CHURCH".

The reason discipleship is comprised of learning and teaching is because whenever you leave the life you have become accustomed to for a new unknown life; there is much information you must learn. Romans 12:2, *"And be not conformed to this world: but be ye transformed by the renewing of your mind, that ye may prove what is that good, and acceptable, and perfect will of God."* Once you begin to learn it then becomes your obligation to teach others. So the next time you wonder why you're not as successful as the next preacher you saw on television, heard on the radio, doing a worldwide book tour, etc. Remember that is not "success" in God's eyes. Success in God's eyes is when you respect and reverence the position of authority God has placed upon you. It's when you use your position to enhance God's people and his kingdom. Success as a spiritual leader is taking someone who comes to know and accept Christ and nurture them to a place of self-sustainability in their own personal relationship with God. Success is doing God's work outside of the four walls of a building; it's going into the shelters, streets, and community to show the love of God as well as teaching them about the God of that love.

7

THE TEACHER

The Teacher is crucial for the existence of disciples and the body of believers because every person that receives salvation obtains redemption based off of a small piece of truth. The fact that Jesus is the son of God; that he walked on the earth to be an example for us, and died to redeem us from sin, and gave us the right to eternal life. Those are foundational truths. That is the small piece of truth that those of us that have been born again into God's kinship knew, understood, and accepted. This truth gave us access to our salvation; but to maintain a godly lifestyle more truth will be needed.

This means that the teacher within us is what introduces others to the knowledge of Christ; which in return leads them to make him Lord and Savior of their life. After salvation the teacher is crucial because the five offices are supposed to operate in unity to ensure that the body of believers have everything that's needed to progress in God's will and purpose for their lives. Individuals come into discipleship with worldly (carnal) values and views that must be traded for godly ones; so the teacher is crucial because they explain the gospel. The teacher office and the pastor office works in conjunction to shape the lives of every believer.

Acts 13:1 tells us, *"Now there were in the church that was at Antioch certain prophets and teachers; as Barnabas, and Simeon that was called Niger, and Lucius of Cyrene, and Manaen, which had been brought up with Herod the tetrarch, and Saul."* The text here is interesting and insightful because even telling you who was present you can see that they were unified in teaching the church at Antioch. We see among the prophets and teachers is a new convert: Manaen, who grew up with "Herod the tetrarch"; the same Herod that sought the life of Jesus as an infant. Manaen was there to be taught how to live his life as a follower and disciple of Jesus Christ. Without the unity of these great men of God; the work in Antioch would not have flourished.

2 Timothy 1:11 says, "*Whereunto I am appointed a preacher, and an apostle, and a teacher of the Gentiles.*" Verses one through eleven tells us that Paul writes this letter to his son in the gospel; Timothy and he is encouraging Timothy to continue strong in the building and progression of the church as he taught him. Timothy is saddened by Paul's incarceration and Paul comforts and exhorts him yet he also pushes him to move forward in leadership. He lets Timothy know that he understands the burden he carries, and although his desire is to be there helping him in the kingdom work; he is more than capable of the job because of the great faith he has and the mantle he released upon him by the laying on of hands. Paul instructs him to stir up the gift of God that is within him to complete the work. He also reminds him that fear is not from

God; but that God has equipped us with love, power, and a sound mind. He tells him to not be ashamed of the testimony of Jesus nor his imprisonment but tells him to relate to his own afflictions experienced through his work in the gospel. Finally, Paul lets Timothy know in verse eleven; that he was appointed in multiple capacities to continue and expand the building of the church by being a preacher, an apostle to the churches but also by being a teacher to the Gentiles (un-believers).

The office of the teacher is never to be taken lightly. It's strange because in the traditions of church and what most of us grew up knowing and understanding; the teacher seemed like the least of the five-fold; when in fact it is the most important piece to salvation. This is why James 3:1 tells us, "Not many of you should become teachers, my fellow believers, because you know that we who teach will be judged more strictly." James points out that anyone walking in the office of a teacher will come under a stricter judgement that others. It is also a hard burden to bear because those who teach must be studios so that they're sharing correct information. The scripture in James 4:17, *"Therefore to him that knoweth to do good, and doeth it not, to him it is sin."* further helps us to understand that the information you know; you are responsible to live. Although Paul's information was meant to show Timothy the key to establishing and continuous building of "The Church". This is still a crucial foundation for disciples and should be the center of our practices even today.

8

THE EVANGELIST

The evangelist is a preacher, a proclaimer of the good news "the gospel" which is the life, death, burial, and resurrection of Jesus Christ. The evangelist speaks to the crowds as well as sharing the message of Jesus one on one as well. The evangelist is full of fire; not because they have more Holy Ghost than others but because their desire is strong and relentless to introduce or present Christ to anyone and everyone that will listen. The evangelist is not just this way with those who don't know God but their just as passionate and relentless in getting already established believers to be more eager to share the gospel with others.

Luke 4:18 says, "[Jesus said] *The spirit of the Lord is upon me, because he hath anointed me to preach the gospel to the poor; he hath sent me to heal the brokenhearted, to preach deliverance to the captives, and recovering of sight to the blind, to set at liberty them that are bruised.*" The Strong's concordance defines "evangelist" as a preacher of the Gospel. The word evangelize means to announce good news. In the scripture we just read it displays Jesus as the supreme evangelist. He is the good news and he was anointed by the Holy Spirit to preach that news here on earth. Jesus evangelized here on earth with great success; he won multitudes to the faith.

None of the apostles operated primarily in that office; they all worked in other areas as well; this may have been because they were the first foundation of the New Testament church and therefore help was limited because everyone coming into salvation had to be disciple. The process is the same for us today but we have more seasoned (spiritually mature, learned, experienced) believers to assist us with the assignment of making and maturing disciples. The harvest is now plenteous but true laborers are few. Leaders must get back to the fundamental principles of making and maturing disciples. In Acts 21:8-9 *"And the next day, we that were in Paul's company departed, and came unto Caesarea: and we entered into the house of Phillip the evangelist, which was one of the seven {deacons in the Jerusalem church}; and abode with him. 9) And the same man had four daughters, virgins, which did prophesy."* In this text we are introduced to the evangelist known as Phillip. In order to understand these offices, it's always a great idea to study those who held the office long before you. Many times this helps believers to establish their spiritual identity and uncover their purpose as well as their placement within the five-fold ministry.

Phillip according to scripture and study was said to be a man full of the Spirit and wisdom of God (1 Timothy 3:13). This reveals that he was a dependable man with solid godly character; he was respected by those who knew and observed him. Philip proved himself to be faithful and effective as a deacon; which is why he gained such an impeccable reputation; and his service as a deacon developed great boldness.

Acts 8:5-16 shows who Phillip was in his operation as an evangelist. The text reveals that Phillip didn't just proclaim the word of God; it shows that he performed signs which caused the people to pay attention to the words that flowed from his lips. Some of the signs people witnessed were evil spirits being cast out and those paralyzed and lame being healed. These signs accompanied with his proclamation of Christ won countless souls to Christ for the end of the text tells us that they were baptized in the name of the Lord Jesus.

Many people believe there's no big difference between a prophet and an evangelist; and depending on who you're asking that may be true; but one sure difference is this; the evangelist message does NOT change. Their message is the gospel of Jesus Christ; every testimony, every side conversation, every missions act done, and every sermon will all be presenting the life, death, burial, and resurrection

of Jesus Christ with the intent and focus of saving lost souls.

9

THE PASTOR

The office of "pastor" has got to be the most glorified office known to man; at least by the standards of traditions, myths, and improper teachings many believers have been made accustomed to. In today's society churches have been plagued by pastors who want to be revered, taken care of, and idolized. These kinds of pastors take from their congregations without giving much back in return. Admiration and the desire to be mentored has turned countless new believers into servants and slaves of men instead of God. No matter the examples you see before you today nor the examples you've encounter throughout your life; these are not the standards for believers called to walk in this ministry office; in fact, it's the very opposite.

The pastor must possess and exhibit love for people. They must have compassion for people and the church. A pastor should have a giving attitude instead of an expectation to receive; how do we know this? We know this because in almost every instance in scripture the pastor is referred to as a shepherd. A shepherd is primarily responsible for the safety and care of the flock. The shepherd is responsible for grazing the animals (leading them in herds to areas of good grass. The shepherd keeps a watchful eye on them as they eat to ensure that they don't eat plants that are poisonous. In my research of the Shepherd I even discovered that most don't take up permanent residence anywhere because the sheep will eventually eat up all of the grass in its area; it's for this cause that they live in mobile homes of some type to be able to move when the sheep have exhausted resources to feed from.

This gave me so much revelations even about who a pastor is and what they do. A pastor must be a selfless individual who's concerned with the well-being of the flock (people) God has assigned him to care for and protect. Jeremiah 3:15 *"And I will give you pastors according to mine heart, which shall feed you with knowledge and understanding."* This is not to say that the pastor should totally abandon himself and needs to care for God's people. I am only emphasizing his obligation and desire to put the flock first. God uses Jeremiah to speak prophetically to His people to let them know that he was going to send a leader that would care for them and impart/teach them of the knowledge and understanding he/she has obtained.

The spiritual pastor is just like the shepherd in almost every sense. In order to protect and care for the flock properly there will be times where he/she must nurture them; there will also be many times where he/she must rebuke and correct them. 2 Timothy 4:2, *"Preach the word; be instant in season, out of season; reprove, rebuke, exhort with all long suffering and doctrine."* That is what the shepherd's staff was used for.

Most times the shepherd could use the hook of the staff to re-direct a wandering sheep; but he never had to beat them into submission because they were humble and obedient; they just required direction.

The last thing I want to add about the pastor may alarm some and anger others; but contrary to popular belief: the pastor is not the ultimate authority within the church body. His/her job is essential for the growth of that flock but those who hold this office tend to operate as if they are the final and ultimate authority of that church body. Nothing cringes a believer's heart more than hearing a pastor go on and on about what will not be said nor done in their church. The pastor is the under shepherd of the church because God himself is the shepherd.

The office of the pastor requires great patience as well as the ability to give careful instruction to the believers within its congregation/body. This is why the scripture tells the flock not to rebuke them. The flock doesn't have the authority to rebuke (correct/chastise) the pastor but there are two other offices that do; the prophet and the apostle. Ezekiel 34:1 *"And the word of the Lord came unto me saying, 2) Son of man, prophesy against the shepherds of Israel, prophesy, and say unto them, Thus saith the Lord God unto the shepherds; Woe be to the shepherds of Israel that do feed themselves! Should not the shepherds feed the flocks? 3) Ye eat the fat, and ye clothe you with the wool, ye kill them that are fed: but ye feed not the flock."* As these scriptures point out; God is angered by a shepherd who doesn't take his responsibility serious. He sends correction and rebuke for pastors who take care of themselves by providing their own needs over those of God's people. This is why pastors have to possess such strong love because they have to be able to meet the flock where they are. In this scripture text God sends the prophet Ezekiel to the shepherds (pastors) of Israel to rebuke them and chastise them because of the wrong they did unto the people.

A true pastor understands their position and place of authority within the church body. They don't take that authority for granted, nor do they use it to tear down or cause infraction to others. They understand the importance of consistently being able to lead the flock to the water source and abundant place nourishment. For this reason, pastors have to be uninhibited by the opinions, finances, and influence of others so they may produce consistent and rich word to the flock; so they can grow and develop appropriately. This is why the teacher and pastor works closely together. It's also the reason why church offices such as; elder, deacon, and bishop/overseer was introduced into the New Testament church, and why we continue in those practices today.

10

THE PROPHET

The word prophet comes from the Hebrew word "nabi" which means; to bubble forth, as from a fountain, "hence to utter". The first person in the bible to be called a prophet was Abraham. This is significant because most people don't pay attention to the fact that God himself called him such. Genesis 20:7, "*Now therefore restore the man his wife; for he is a prophet, and he shall pray for thee, and thou shalt live: and if thou restore her not, know thou that thou shalt surely die, thou, and all that are thine.*" We see that God tells the prince that took Abraham's wife that he is a prophet who has the ability to save his life through his prayers; he warns the man that not returning her will result in his death. This scripture text also gives us insight into the calling of a prophet. A prophet cannot be called or commissioned by man or even the church;

he/she must be called by God himself; the meaning is simple for if you choose someone to carry your important messages wouldn't you be the one to choose that person? You would want to make sure the person was able to carry even the most personal of messages without telling anyone other than its intended recipients, you would want to know that the person had the ability to repeat exactly what you said among other qualities right? God is the same way; he doesn't choose just anyone to carry his messages.

Many God appointed prophets were chosen after Abraham and they came from all walks of life. A person's background does not qualify nor disqualify them from being used by God to do great and mighty things. There are so many leaders in the faith that were chosen from peculiar situations. Moses was drawn from the river and raised in the palace of pharaoh. He was given an education, culture, and lived a life of material pleasantries yet he was born from the womb of a slave during a time where his adopted family sought to destroy the promise of a deliverer; who just happen to be him. Despite all of the luxuries and despite how easy it would have been for him to remain in comfortability; he answered the call of God no matter how reluctant he was in the beginning.

Like Moses; many that are called into the office of prophet feel the constant sense of unworthiness. God even has to comfort Jeremiah when he was called at the age of fifteen to be his prophet. Jeremiah 1:5-7 *"Before I formed thee in the belly I knew thee; and before thou camest forth out of the womb I sanctified thee, and I ordained thee a prophet unto the nations. 6) Then said I, Ah, Lord God! Behold, I cannot speak: for I am a child. 7) But the Lord said unto me, Say not, I am a child: for thou shalt go to all that I send thee, and whatsoever I command thee thou shalt speak."* Jeremiah was afraid of what the people would say, if they would receive him or not, etc. God will reassure us just as he did with Jeremiah when he says in the next verse; do not be afraid of their faces: for I am with thee. Everyone will not be receptive of the prophetic words nor the authority of the prophet's office; yet this cannot be an excuse to not do what God has called them to do.

Prophets must be obedient to God. They must have an intimate personal relationship with God to ensure that their direct line to Him is not tampered with nor blocked. The office of prophet comes with an authority released over the individual to speak on God's behalf. So there are some clear operations of the prophet that we need to recap on. The first operations is they are called by God alone. The second is that God gives the specific message and the designated audience the message is for. The third observance is that most often the prophets message was one of correction and even judgement. A message of blessing or prosperity was so rare in fact that when God instructed Jonah to go to Nineveh he was sure the message was of doom; but instead it was a message of forgiveness and hope.

Jonah's response to God's message for Nineveh brings a whole other warning for the prophet. A prophet must be careful not to mistake their emotions, thoughts, and feelings to be those of God. Jonah's emotions almost cost his life and his prophetic authority with God. Prophets must always remember that God is God even to our enemies and if he has called you to serve His purpose; many times it will conflict with your feelings and thoughts; because prophecy isn't personal like other areas of ministry; it is a three-step process of delivering God's messages. A prophet must be able to first hear the message of God. This can be in various different ways; Abraham was visited by angels and given instruction, Moses heard the audible voice of God (on the mountain and even from the burning bush), Joseph dreamed dreams (that he at first didn't even know how to interpret), Ezekiel saw visions, and Samuel heard the voice of his spiritual father and teacher.

The prophet is not confined to a specific message or method. There's a lot of debate on the relevancy and need for the prophet in today's society. This is understandable but very false. Most of these opinions occur because the Old Testament prophet existed and operated during a time where the Holy Spirit was not yet freely given to all men; so it is clearly understood why God needed someone to be his voice. Most people believe that now because of the Holy Spirit that lives within believers that whatever God needs to say can be done through his spirit within us directly. This is a true statement. God can speak a word to us through His spirit but reality tells us that we are not always receptive of God's messages. Some messages are harder than others to receive. Some people turn deaf ears to the correction God sends through his word, through his ministers, and even through speaking directly to us. In these moments we need a prophet. Someone who has no personal stake in the message; a person who has been in the presence of God and knows his voice without wavering. Someone who has no idea what you're dealing and struggling with. The prophetic is still among the signs and wonders that show people the truth and accuracy

of God's power and presence in the earth.

11

THE APOSTLE

The office of the apostle is the foundation of the church. They were responsible for not only proclaiming God's revelation but for teaching the new truth the church needed to flourish. Both the apostle and prophet had a hand in building the early church by giving us the word of God (writing the scriptures through divine inspiration from God). The scripture writings of the New testament prophets and apostles equipped the church with every fundamental piece of information they needed to know.

The new testament apostles walked directly with Jesus on the earth except for the apostle Paul; who was led directly by God through the indwelling of the Holy Spirit (we'll talk more about this significance a little later in this chapter). The first twelve apostles were men handpicked by Jesus himself after already walking with him as disciples "students". Jesus walked with them closely; he taught them vital life lessons; imparted wisdom, boldness, and compassion unto them, and was a daily example of what kingdom living should look like. Jesus was preparing the Apostles to build and carry on "THE CHURCH" within the earth after His death and resurrection.

Luke 6:12-13 *"And it came to pass in those days, that he went out into a mountain to pray, and continued all night in prayer to God. 13) And when it was day, he called unto him his disciples: and of them he chose twelve, whom also he named apostles;"*. If you continue reading this chapter you see the revelation that Jesus had more than that twelve disciples he had many but he knew that all of them could not lead and build the church after he was gone; so, after consulting in prayer with His father; Jesus chose the twelve that would be able to do the work of an apostle.

The function of the apostle is to establish, train, and govern the body of believers as well as the physical church. The apostles were to guide pastors in church operations to ensure that they kept the purpose and presence of God as its main focus with the assignment of winning souls and making disciples at its core. Although the early apostles operated primarily as a teacher, evangelist to build the early churches; they did not stay on as pastors of the local bodies. The apostles appointed disciples that showed their stability and faithfulness to God as well as their dedication and ability to learn and live godly lifestyles.

Let's examine the relationship between the apostle Paul and Timothy. We're first introduced to Timothy within Acts 16 as Paul is heading out on his second missionary journey. Paul brings Timothy with him at first as an apprentice. Their relationship then evolves and Paul becomes his spiritual father. In 1 Timothy 1:2 we can clearly see the father/son relationship, *"Unto Timothy, my own son in the faith: Grace, mercy, and peace, from God our Father and Jesus Christ our Lord.*" Then Paul becomes a mentor and a witness for Timothy. 2 Timothy 3:10-11 "*But thou hast fully known my doctrine, manner of life, purpose, faith, longsuffering, charity, patience, 11) Persecutions, afflictions, which came unto me at Antioch, at Iconium, at Lystra; what persecutions I endured: but out of them all the Lord delivered me.*" Finally, Paul no longer refers to him as a student nor a son; he now introduces him as a partner/co-laborer. As you continue to study you will find that Paul leaves Timothy in charge of the church of Ephesus because Paul was concerned about the false teaching that was going on there. Timothy was given apostolic rights within that church; for Paul instructed him to resurrect specific church offices to help run the established and growing church. However, they needed Timothy there to continue teaching the truth to prevent the flock from being misled. This interaction between Paul and Timothy allow us to observe several things. We first observe that leadership within the local physical church assemblies should be established by apostolic order. Leaders then should be trained apostolically to serve that assembly, and then a pastor should be left to continue the work. Paul did not abandon the churches he and the other apostles started; he frequently visited them all to check on their progress and to correct any issues that may have been out of order. This is why the apostolic office is known as the church's "government".

It's interesting that many believe the apostle like the prophet are no longer in operation. It is the belief of many that Jesus only intended the fivefold to establish and build the New Testament churches and the now that the foundation of the church has been established through the word of God; we no longer need men to do foundational work. However, what we saw take place within the New Testament was merely a plan of action for the church today. As long as churches are being formed; there will always be a need for the full operation of the five-fold ministry.

Apostle Paul is revered as one of the greatest apostles ever; partly because his call was different from the original twelve. Paul was the only one of the establishing apostles that did not walk with Jesus; and even though he did not have the same advantage in that area as the other apostles his call and discipleship is what gave him the greatness needed to resurrect the New Testament church.

Paul was uniquely equipped for the work of an apostle. He was disciple by the Holy Spirit directly. He had no man teacher; because of his background as well as his experience with God on the Damascus road; Paul was not wavering in his faith and belief in God. After his three-day blindness Paul moved full throttle into ministry with the guidance, power, and authority of the Holy Spirit. Paul worked in the marketplace to fund his missionary journey's. He preached and thousands were saved and baptized with the Holy Ghost, he made countless disciples, and trained many of them to be great leaders. Paul understood how to obey God's instructions without fail, he understood the value in unifying with other leaders to establish, build, and maintain. Paul was a great leader. He was full of the power and authority of God. He operated in a sense of urgency to preach and teach the truth of Jesus to bring others into salvation. Many believe that his urgency, boldness, and intensity was a result of him seeking redemption for the countless believer's lives he took before his conversion. It's a clear reminder to us all that we should always remain humble and grateful for the lifestyles we were rescued out from; and that in return should fuel our desire to see others free. One of the things I personally love about the apostle Paul is the fact that although he was mentored by the Holy Spirit directly; at some point he went to meet with the original twelve. In his meeting with the twelve apostles he shares with them all that the Holy Spirit taught him and instructed him to do. He did this to make sure that he was in sync with the true foundation of Jesus. He understood that he was working with the original apostles to build upon Jesus' foundation and he allowed himself to be held accountable by those who knew and had been taught by Jesus personally. He understood that any differences in teaching would cause a riff within the churches. Paul did not operate solely from his zeal; he operated out of the will and wisdom of God.

Paul should be a perfect example to every disciple of Jesus in today's age because he was the first apostle to operate from the leading of the Holy Spirit. It is important that all who receive salvation continue learning who God is and what he expects from us. It is equally important to understand that every spirit filled believer has been commissioned to work in one if not several areas of the five-fold ministry. We refer to disciples by their title to emphasize their area of ministry function and focus; not to glorify them; not to inflate their ego's; and especially not to say they're greater than other believers. When the people of God truly allow themselves to be governed by the plan Jesus provided is when we'll find the state of the physical assembly better and functioning as it was intended to function. This will require every disciple of Jesus Christ to continue learning about his character and his plan; while being determined to show the example of it within the fibers of their everyday lives.

12

CHURCH OFFICES

The last subject we will cover is church offices. We must clearly define the difference between church offices and the fivefold ministry offices. A church office is an appointment by an apostle or pastor (which is the governmental and organizational structure of the physical church assembly). Church offices were created by the apostles to assist the physical church assemblies in their spiritual growth as well as its organization and administrative practices. Church officers ensured that the Pastor of that particular assembly was able to meet the spiritual needs and address the natural needs of the members of the assembly. This in no means defame the church officer's roles; because they typically do some of the same functions of the pastor. This is why it's important for even church roles to be held by spirit filled believers. Titus 1:4-5,

"To Titus, mine own son after the common faith: Grace, mercy, and peace from God the Father and the Lord Jesus Christ our Saviour. 5) For this cause left I thee in Crete, that thou shouldest set in order the things that are wanting, and ordain elders in every city, as I had appointed thee:". Apostle Paul instructs Titus just as he previously instructed Timothy; to ordain elders to assist him with the shepherding of the churches in Crete.

There are three church offices that Paul instructed to be created to assist with the work of the physical church assembly. The Pastor was considered to be the senior leader and all other church offices answered to him and received their instructions from him; but their function was to serve God's people with compassion, knowledge, wisdom, godly character, integrity, and most of all truth. The three church offices are: the elder; the deacon; and the bishop. Church offices are not spiritually assigned by God like the fivefold offices. Church offices are assigned by the pastor that leads the assembly or even the apostle that established the assembly. 1 Timothy 3:1-13 gives us a full spectrum of requirements for individuals seeking or appointed to the office of a bishop or deacon. Bible scholars believe that both the bishop and elder were similar functions within the local assembly. The word bishop is translated as "overseer" which is why many assume that they govern over churches as an apostle but the truth is; a pastor who is in charge of multiple assemblies can appoint elders, deacons, or bishops to assist in the day to day functions of leadership within the church. These offices are much like our present day: assistant and co-pastors. That is why those chosen for these duties had to be of particular character. According to the scripture text; a bishop must be: blameless, the husband of one wife, vigilant, sober, of good behavior, given to hospitality, and able to teach. He also couldn't be struggling with or susceptible to; drinking wine, getting into fights, greedy for gain, jealous of what others have. A bishop must instead be patient, rule his own home well (this includes raising children that were well behaved and obedient to his rule), had to have a good reputation outside of the assembly as well as within it. These qualifications were basic necessity for those who would be leading or helping to lead the local church assembly in the will and ways of God. And since lifestyle is a key example of the power of God working within us to help transform our lives it is important to choose leaders who will not cause strife amongst the body nor speak or commit offenses that will damage, block, or interrupt the faith and progress of disciples within the flock.

The qualifications listed for deacons in Timothy 3:8-13; imply that they performed many important services within the local assembly as well. However, it seems that the deacon's functions were more along the lines of actual physical service of the church. They were normally the ones responsible for visiting the sick and administering funds to help widows, orphans, and others in need within the assembly. They were also responsible for administering the Lord's Supper. It is an honor to serve the local assembly and in such perilous times were people do not want to go into churches because of the hurt, misappropriation of funds, false teaching, and selfish ambitious being displayed before them. Many have lost faith in the church assembly; including some believers. Although we understand why people feel this way; it is not acceptable to teach against the church assembly; because it is still a much needed tool in making and strengthening disciples. What our assignment and goals must be; is to raise up real church assemblies that mirror the foundations that Jesus laid for the church. The goal is to not stop attending church; but rather to become the true church.

The true church assembly that follows Jesus' plan and foundation will always represent the church that Jesus spoke about in Matthew 16:18, "*And I say also unto thee, That thou art*

Peter, and upon this rock I will build my church; and the gates of hell

shall not prevail against it."

www.ingramcontent.com/pod-product-compliance
Lightning Source LLC
Chambersburg PA
CBHW071103090426
42737CB00013B/2449